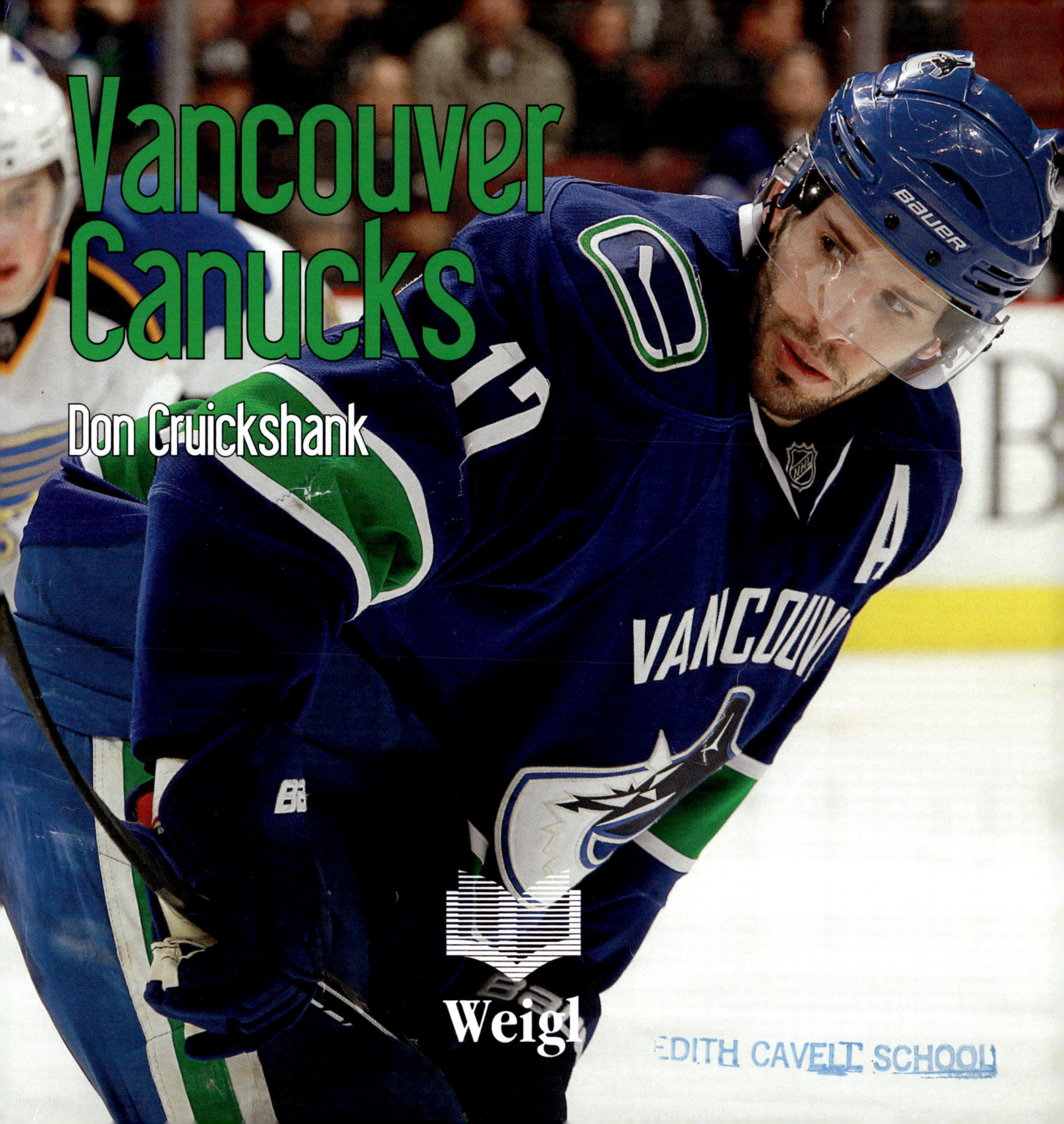

Vancouver Canucks

Don Cruickshank

Weigl

The publisher wishes to thank the Hoffart Family for inspiring this series.

Published by Weigl Educational Publishers Limited
6325 10th Street SE
Calgary, AB T2H 2Z9
Website: www.weigl.ca

Copyright ©2012 Weigl Educational Publishers Limited
All rights reserved. No part of this publication may be reproduced, stored in a retrieval system, or transmitted in any form or by any means, electronic, mechanical, photocopying, recording, or otherwise, without the prior written permission of the publisher.

Library and Archives Canada Cataloguing in Publication
Cruickshank, Don, 1977-
         Vancouver Canucks / Don Cruickshank.
(Hockey in Canada)
Includes index.
ISBN 978-1-77071-645-2 (bound).--ISBN 978-1-77071-659-9 (pbk.)
         1. Vancouver Canucks (Hockey team)--Juvenile literature.
I. Title. II. Series: Cruickshank, Don, 1977- . Hockey in Canada.
GV848.V35C775 2011   j796.962'640971133   C2011-900793-2

Printed in the United States of America in North Mankato, Minnesota
1 2 3 4 5 6 7 8 9 0   15 14 13 12 11

072011
WEP040711

Project Coordinator Aaron Carr
Art Director Terry Paulhus

Weigl acknowledges Getty Images as its primary image supplier for this title.

Every reasonable effort has been made to trace ownership and to obtain permission to reprint copyright material. The publisher would be pleased to have any errors or omissions brought to their attention so they may be corrected in subsequent printings.

We acknowledge the financial support of the Government of Canada through the Canada Book Fund for our publishing activities.

CONTENTS

5   Canucks History
7   Home Arena
9   The Jerseys
11   Goalie Masks

13   The Coaches
15   The Mascot
17   Canucks Records
18   Legendary Canucks

20   Star Canucks
22   Unforgettable Moments
23   Brain Teasers
24   Glossary/Index

4

Canucks History

In 1970, Vancouver was awarded a **National Hockey League (NHL)** team. The Canucks were the 13th team to join the NHL. The Buffalo Sabres also joined the NHL that year.

In 1975, the Canucks won their **division** for the first time. They finished the regular season with 86 points. It was also the first time in their history the Canucks made the playoffs. Vancouver has won their division nine times.

The Canucks have played in three Stanley Cup finals, in 1982, 1994, and 2011.

6

Home Arena

The first home **arena** of the Canucks was the Pacific Coliseum. In 1995, the team moved into General Motors Place. Today, it is called Rogers Arena. This arena has a **capacity** of about 18,630 for Canucks games.

In February 2010, Rogers Arena transformed into Canada Hockey Place for the Winter Olympic Games. Both the Canadian men's and women's hockey teams won gold medals in this arena.

More than 17 million people have attended events at Rogers Arena.

7

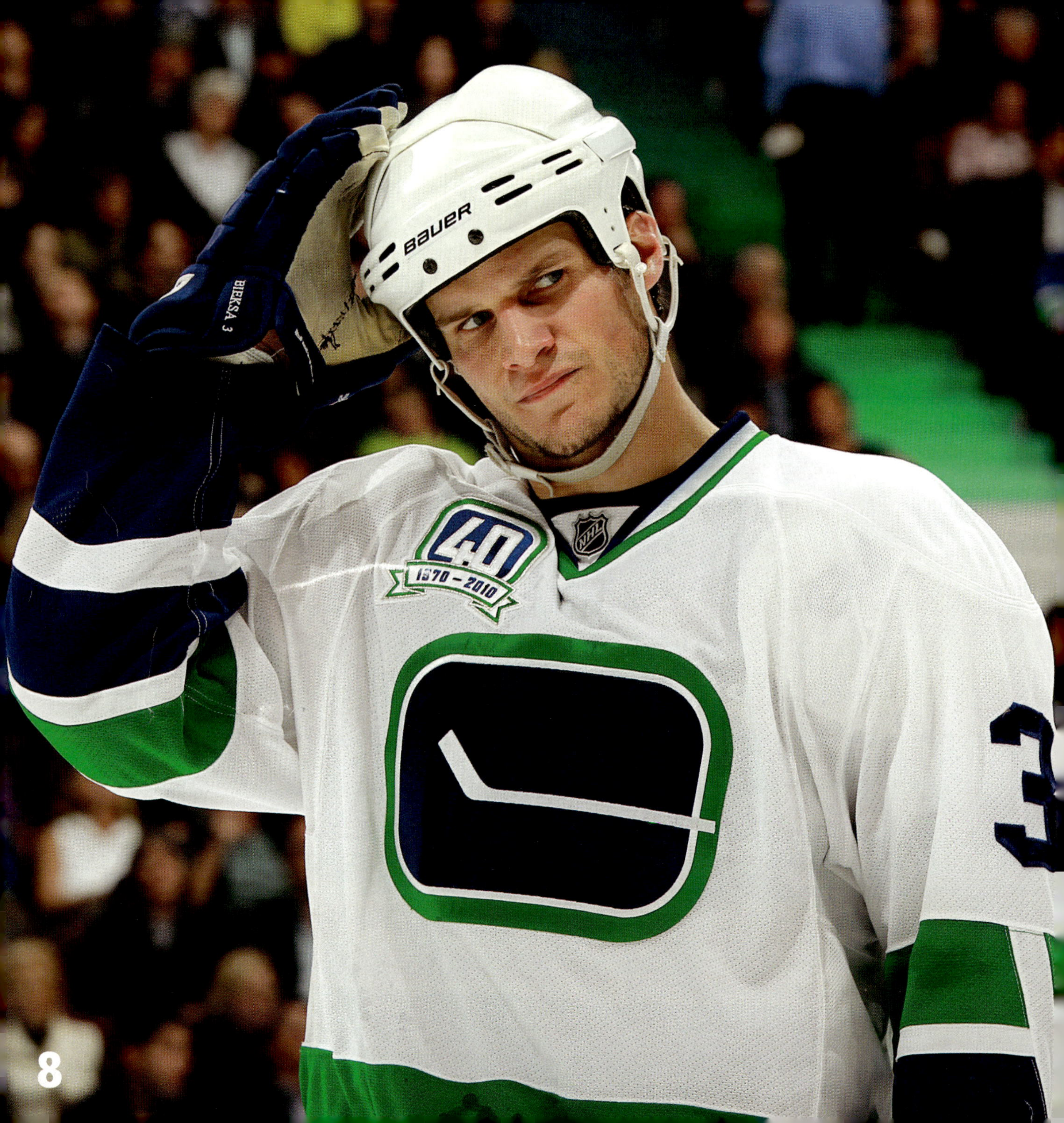
BAUER
BIEKSA 3
40
1970 – 2010
NHL
3

The Jerseys

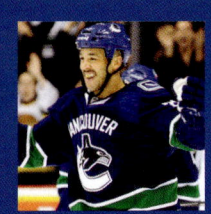

The home jersey is blue with green and white trim. The **orca** on the front became the team's **logo** in 1997.

The away jersey is white with green and blue trim. They have worn these home and away jerseys since 2007.

The third jersey has a hockey rink with a hockey stick inside of it. The stick and the rink form a letter 'C'.

The third jersey is the same style of jersey Vancouver wore in 1970.

10

Goalie Masks

Kirk McLean painted his mask black, orange, and yellow. These were the Canucks' colours for almost 20 years.

Gary Bromley was called "Bones" because he was small. His goalie mask was painted to represent his nickname.

Dan Cloutier wore an older style of mask for most of his career. He had the Canucks' logo painted on the side.

Roberto Luongo has changed his mask design more than 10 times.

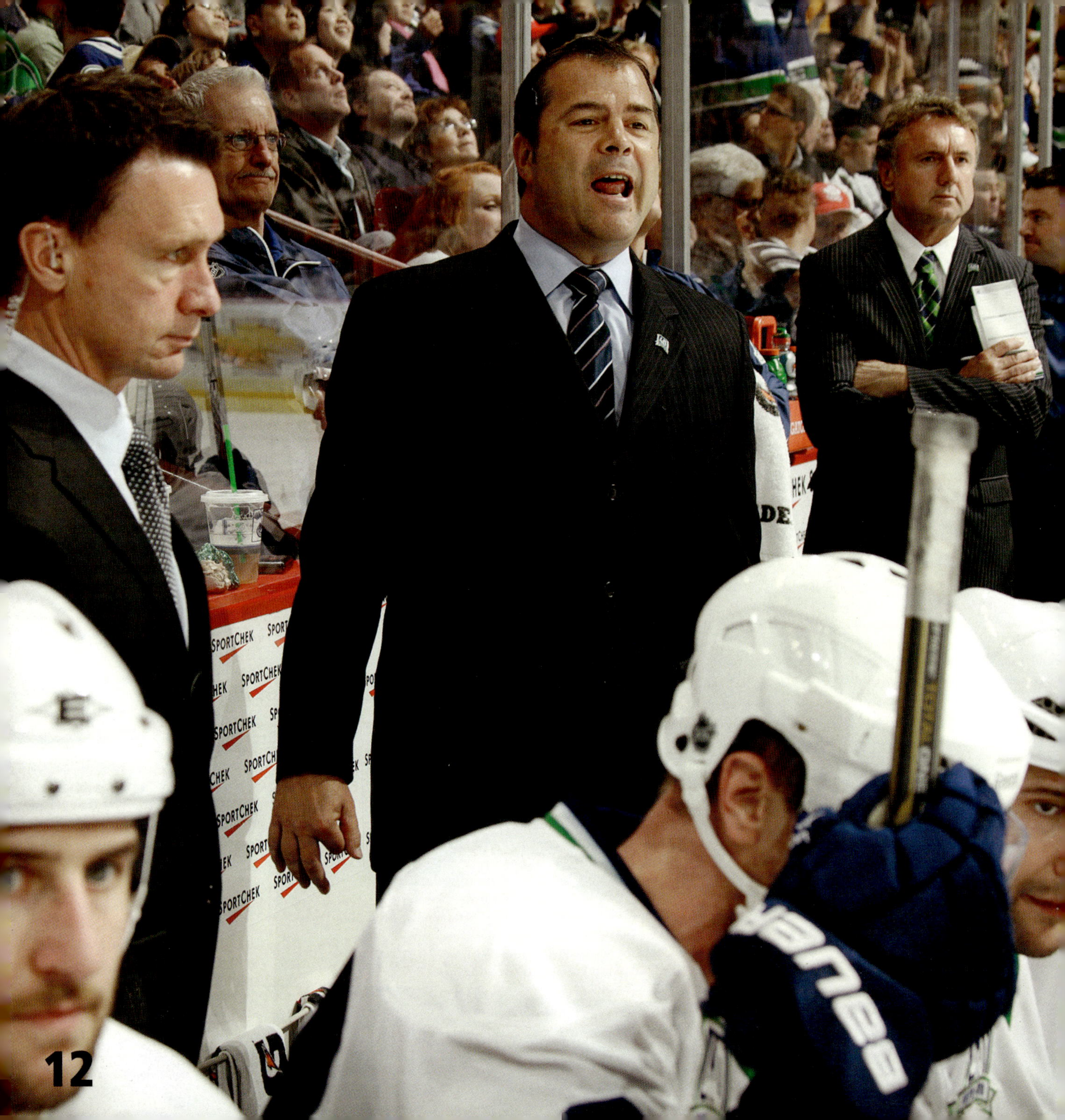
SPORTCHEK

The Coaches

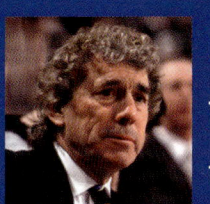

Roger Neilson only coached Vancouver for a short time, but he took the team to its first **Stanley Cup** final in 1982.

Pat Quinn coached the Canucks to the Stanley Cup final in 1994. He coached five different NHL teams in 30 years.

Marc Crawford was with the team for seven seasons. They won 246 games and made the playoffs four times.

Alain Vigneault is the first Canucks coach to reach 50 wins in a season.

14

The Mascot

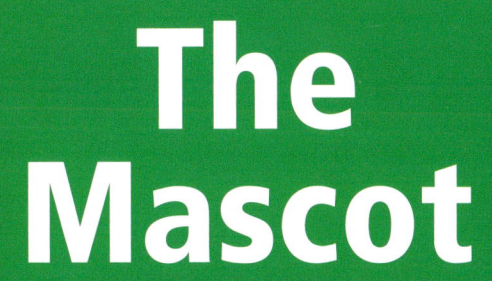

Vancouver's **mascot** is named Fin. He is an orca. Fin gets the Vancouver crowd pumped up during games and teases the other NHL teams. He also pretends to bite people's heads.

For several years, Fin has played in the Celebrity Mascot Games. He competes in events against mascots from other sports leagues. The event raises money to grant wishes for sick children.

Fin can spray mist from his blowhole, and he launches t-shirts into the crowd.

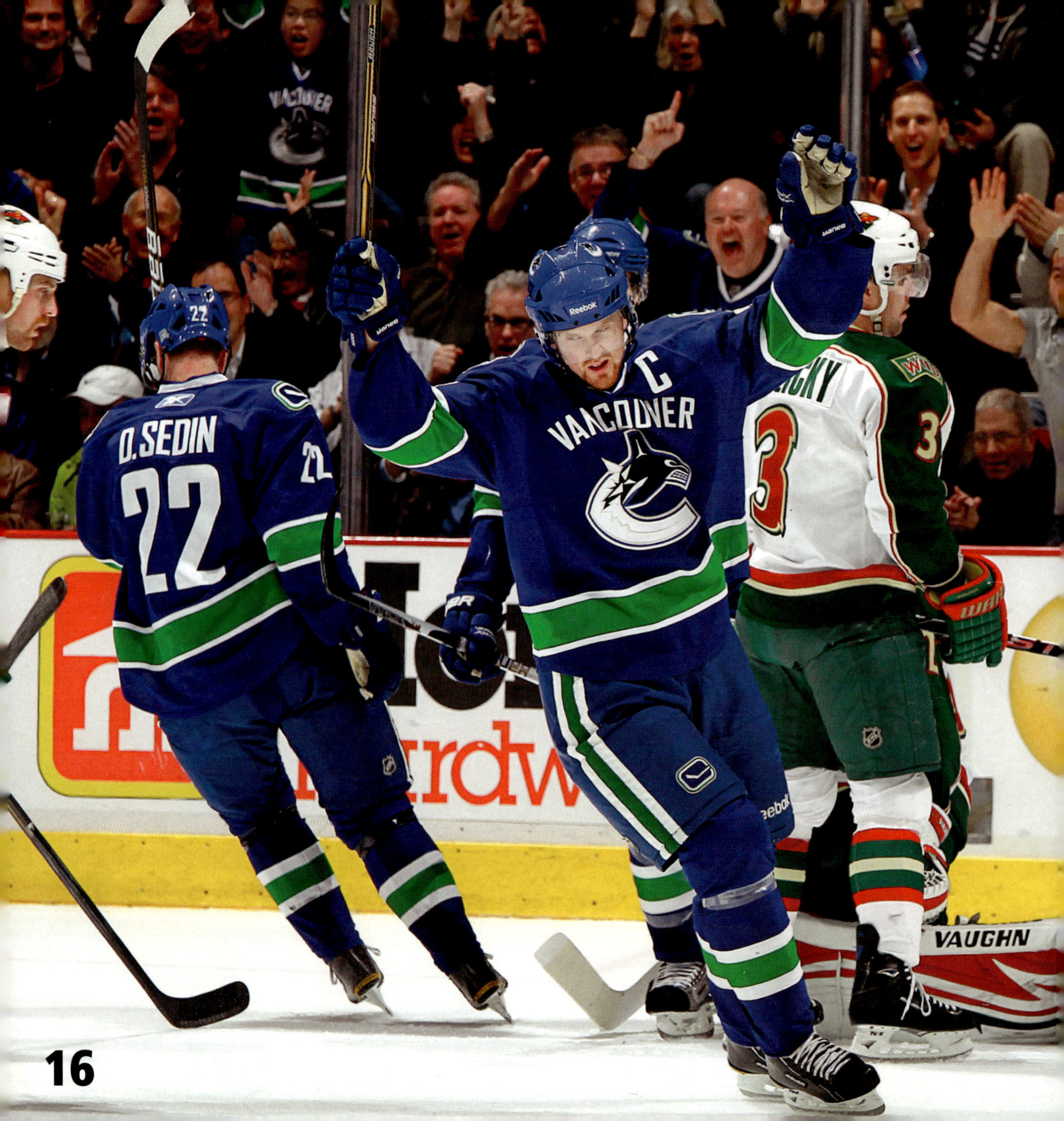
D.SEDIN
22
VANCOUVER
C
3
Reebok
VAUGHN

Canucks Records

CANUCKS ALL-TIME LEADERS

Most Goals
Markus Naslund
346 goals

Most Games Played
Trevor Linden
1,140 games played

Most Penalty Minutes
Gino Odjick
2,127 penalty minutes

Most Assists
Henrik Sedin
504 assists

Most Points
Markus Naslund
756 points

Most Goaltender Wins
Kirk McLean
211 wins

Legendary Canucks

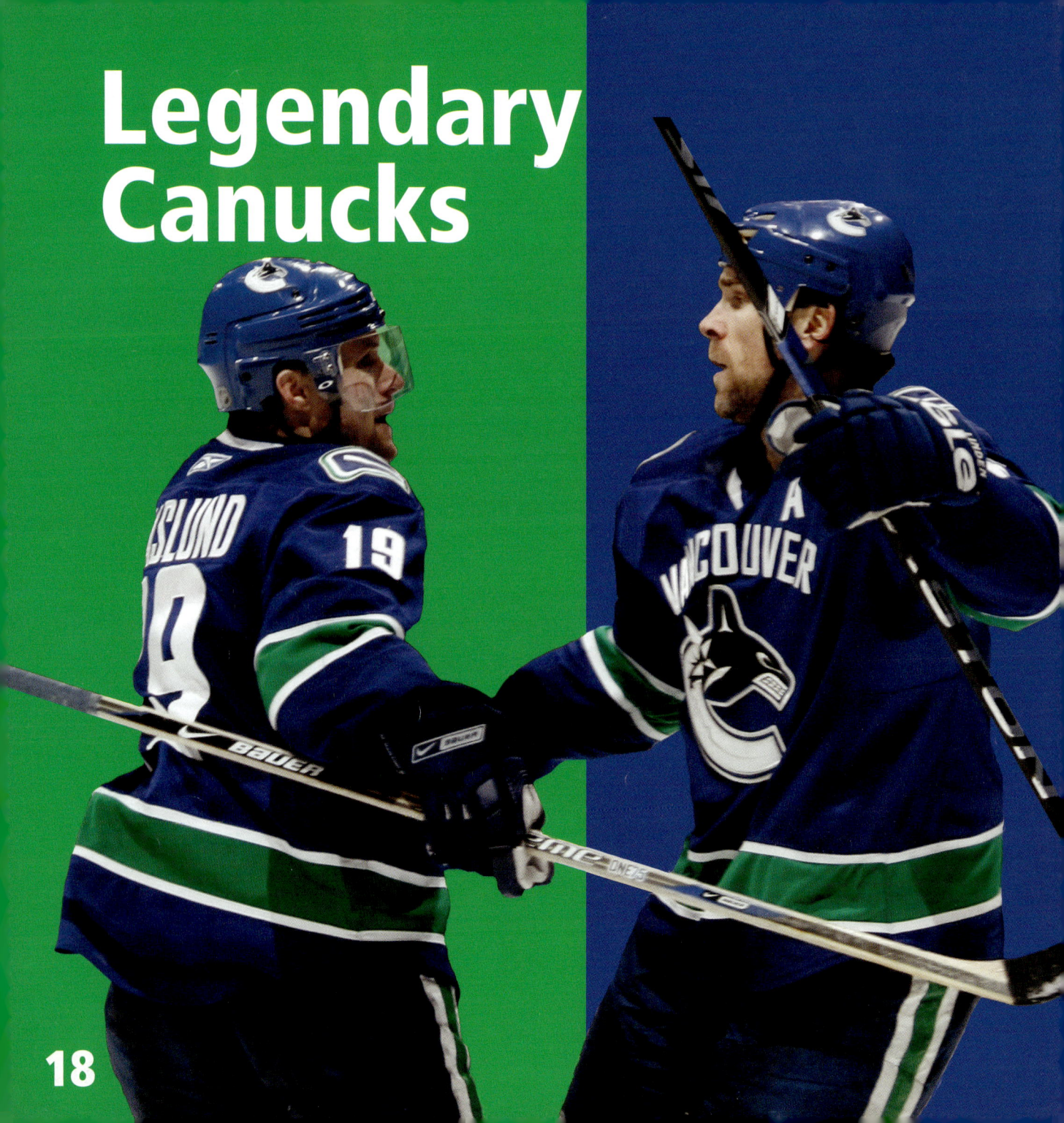

#19 MARKUS NASLUND

Position: Left Wing
Seasons with Canucks: 12
Born: July 30, 1973
Hometown: Ornskoldsvik, Sweden

CAREER FACTS

The Pittsburgh Penguins drafted Markus Naslund in the 1991 **NHL entry draft**. In 1996, he was traded to the Canucks. In the 2002–2003 season, Naslund was second in NHL scoring, with 104 points. That year, he was voted the **Most Valuable Player (MVP)** by other NHL players. Naslund was Vancouver's team captain from 2000 to 2008. He played one season with the New York Rangers in 2009–2010. He retired in 2010.

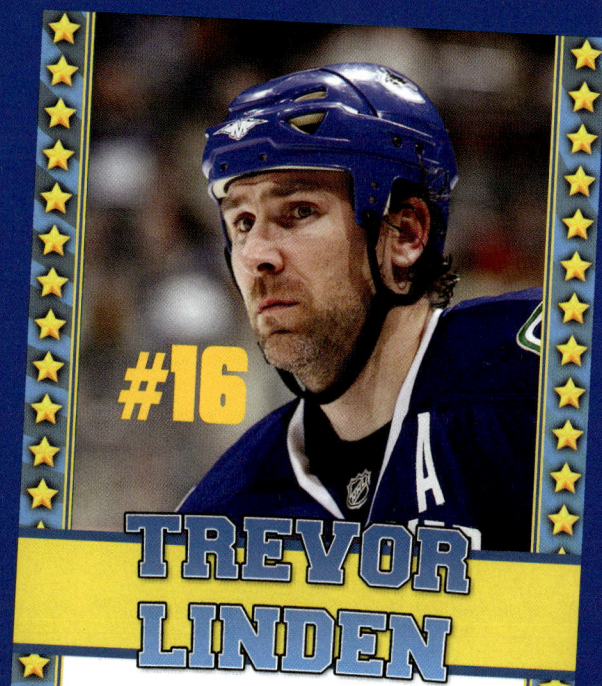

#16 TREVOR LINDEN

Position: Centre
Seasons with Canucks: 16
Born: April 11, 1970
Hometown: Medicine Hat, Alberta

CAREER FACTS

Trevor Linden was drafted second overall by the Canucks in 1988. He played almost 10 seasons with the Canucks before being traded to the New York Islanders. Linden played for two other teams before returning to Vancouver in 2001. He was captain of the Canucks from 1990 to 1997 and retired as a member of the Vancouver Canucks in 2008. In 1,382 career NHL games, Linden scored a total of 867 points.

Star Canucks

#1 ROBERTO LUONGO

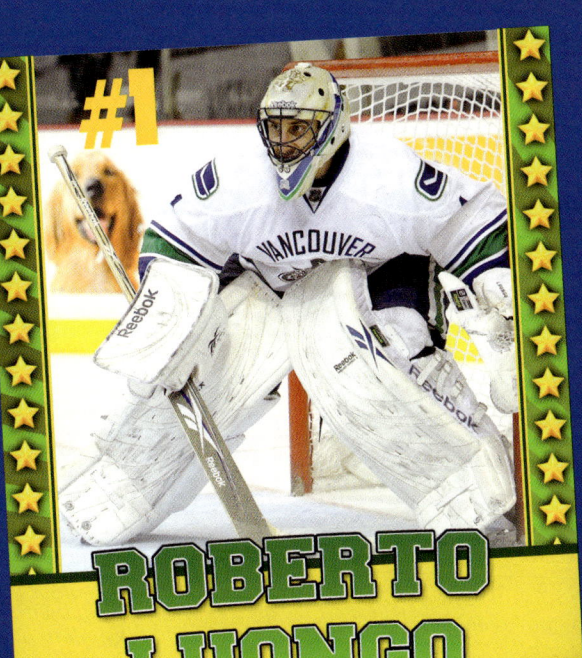

Position: Goaltender
Seasons with Canucks: 5
Born: April 4, 1979
Hometown: Montreal, Quebec

CAREER FACTS

Roberto Luongo was drafted in 1997 by the New York Islanders. After one year, he was traded to the Florida Panthers. In the 2003–2004 season, he set an NHL record for most saves in a season with 2,303. Luongo joined Vancouver in 2006. In 2008, he was named team captain. He was the seventh goalie to be named team captain in NHL history and the first since 1948. He is currently second on the Canucks all-time list for goalie wins.

#22 #33 DANIEL & HENRIK SEDIN

Position: Left Wing & Centre
Seasons with Canucks: 10
Born: September 26, 1980
Hometown: Ornskoldsvik, Sweden

CAREER FACTS

Daniel and Henrik Sedin were both drafted by the Canucks in 1999. The twins have played on the same line since they were young. In the 2009–2010 season, Henrik led the NHL in assists, with 83, and in points, with 112. He was named the league MVP. After that season, Henrik was named team captain. The next season, Daniel led the NHL in points. The brothers rank fourth and fifth on the Canucks all-time scoring list.

Unforgettable Moments

1970
On October 9, the Canucks play their first NHL home game. It is a sellout crowd of 15,564 fans. The Canucks lose, but win their first NHL game two days later.

1992
Pavel Bure scores 60 points in 65 games. He wins the NHL's **rookie** of the year award. The next season, the "Russian Rocket" becomes the first Vancouver player to score 60 goals in a season.

1994
The Canucks advance to the Stanley Cup final for a second time. They lose the series to the New York Rangers in seven games.

1982
The Canucks win their first playoff series and make it all the way to the Stanley Cup final. They lose to the New York Islanders in four games. When the team returns home to Vancouver, about 100,000 fans hold a parade to celebrate the team's effort.

2011
The Canucks finish the regular season as the top team in the NHL. This earns Vancouver their first President's Trophy. In the playoffs, the Canucks advance to the Stanley Cup final for the first time since 1994. They lose to the Boston Bruins in seven games.

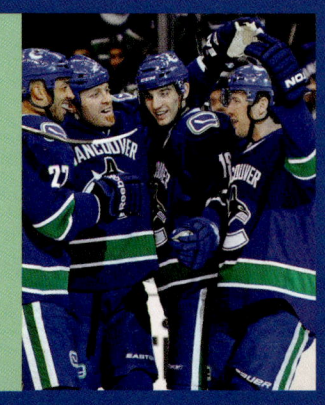

Brain Teasers

Test your knowledge of the Vancouver Canucks by trying to answer these brain teasers.

1. How many times have the Vancouver Canucks won their division?

2. What years did the Canucks play for the Stanley Cup?

3. What type of animal is the Canucks' mascot?

4. What was the Canucks' arena called during the 2010 Winter Olympics?

5. Which Canucks' player has scored the most goals?

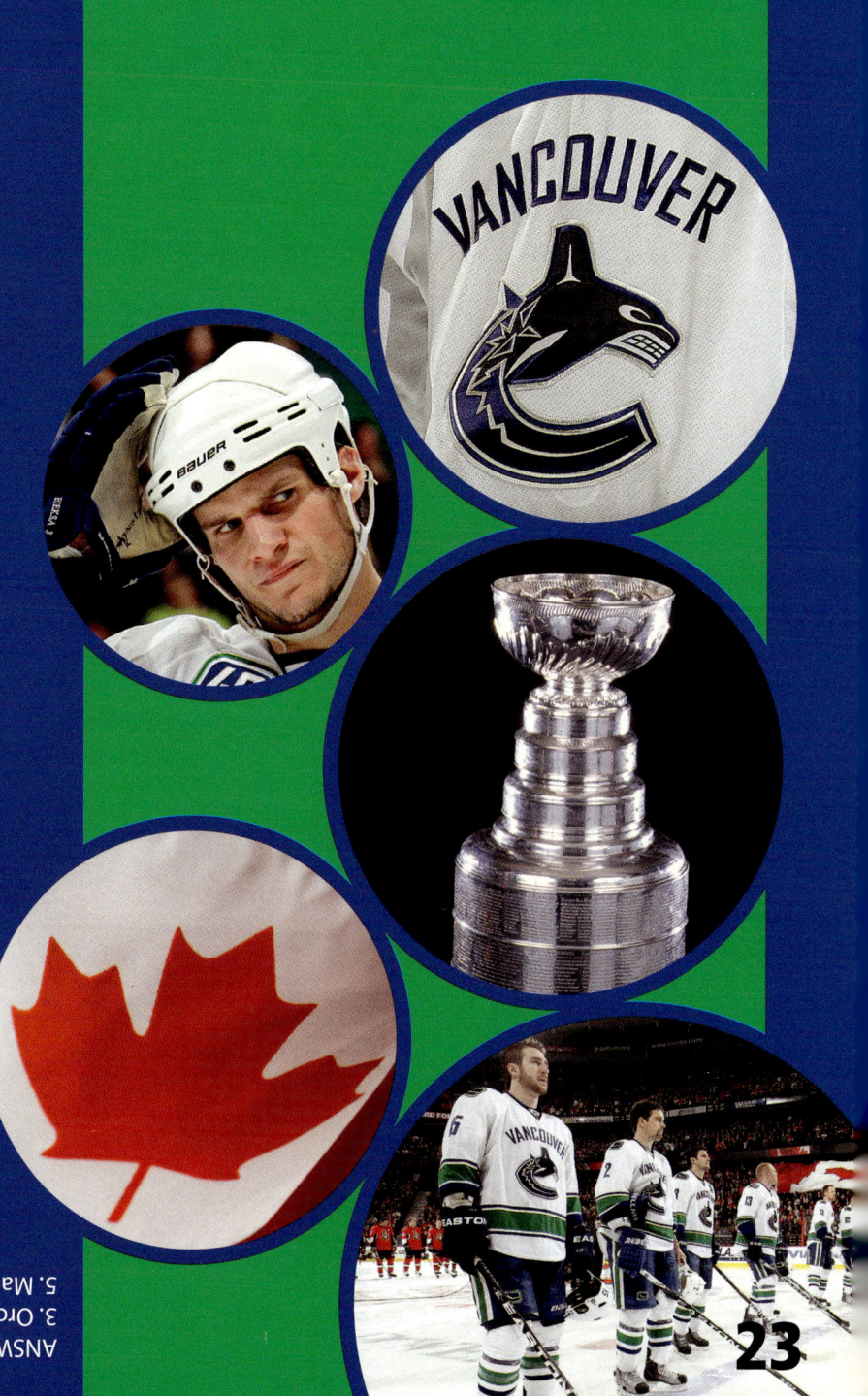

ANSWERS: 1. Nine 2. 1982, 1994, and 2011 3. Orca, or killer whale 4. Canada Hockey Place 5. Markus Naslund

23

Glossary

arena: a building where sports teams play their games

capacity: the maximum number of people that can fit in a stadium

division: a small group of teams that are part of the NHL

logo: a symbol that identifies a team

mascot: an animal or object used to bring a team good luck

Most Valuable Player (MVP): the player judged to be the most important to his team's success

National Hockey League (NHL): an organization for professional hockey teams

NHL entry draft: when NHL teams select junior hockey players to join their organizations

orca: a killer whale

rookie: a player in his or her first season

Stanley Cup: the National Hockey League's trophy for the winner of the playoffs

Index

arena 7, 23

coach 13

jersey 9

Linden, Trevor 17, 19
Luongo, Roberto 11, 21

mascot 15, 23
mask 11

Naslund, Markus 17, 19, 23
National Hockey League (NHL) 5, 13, 15, 19, 21, 22

Sedin, Daniel and Henrik 17, 21
Stanley Cup 5, 13, 22, 23

Vancouver 5, 9, 13, 15, 19, 21, 22, 23

24